Opportunities in Strengthening Trade Assistance

A Report of the CSIS Congressional Task Force on Trade Capacity Building

COCHAIRS
Representative Charles W. Boustany Jr. (R-LA)
Representative Jared S. Polis (D-CO)

PRINCIPAL AUTHORS
Scott Miller
Daniel F. Runde

CONTRIBUTING AUTHORS
Charles Rice
Christina M. Perkins

February 2015

CSIS | CENTER FOR STRATEGIC & INTERNATIONAL STUDIES

ROWMAN & LITTLEFIELD

Lanham • Boulder • New York • London

About CSIS

For over 50 years, the Center for Strategic and International Studies (CSIS) has worked to develop solutions to the world's greatest policy challenges. Today, CSIS scholars are providing strategic insights and bipartisan policy solutions to help decisionmakers chart a course toward a better world.

CSIS is a nonprofit organization headquartered in Washington, D.C. The Center's 220 full-time staff and large network of affiliated scholars conduct research and analysis and develop policy initiatives that look into the future and anticipate change.

Founded at the height of the Cold War by David M. Abshire and Admiral Arleigh Burke, CSIS was dedicated to finding ways to sustain American prominence and prosperity as a force for good in the world. Since 1962, CSIS has become one of the world's preeminent international institutions focused on defense and security; regional stability; and transnational challenges ranging from energy and climate to global health and economic integration.

Former U.S. senator Sam Nunn has chaired the CSIS Board of Trustees since 1999. Former deputy secretary of defense John J. Hamre became the Center's president and chief executive officer in 2000.

CSIS does not take specific policy positions; accordingly, all views expressed herein should be understood to be solely those of the author(s).

ISBN: 978-1-4422-4074-2 (pb); 978-1-4422-4075-9 (eBook)

Center for Strategic & International Studies
1616 Rhode Island Avenue, NW
Washington, DC 20036
202-887-0200 | www.csis.org

Rowman & Littlefield
4501 Forbes Boulevard
Lanham, MD 20706
301-459-3366 | www.rowman.com

| Contents

| Acknowledgments

This report is the product of the Bipartisan Congressional Task Force on Trade Capacity Building, convened by the Project on U.S. Leadership in Development (USLD) and the Scholl Chair in International Business at the Center for Strategic and International Studies (CSIS). The work of USLD would not be possible without Chevron's generous support.

We are grateful to Kaitlin Sighinolfi in the office of Rep. Charles Boustany and Eve Lieberman in the office of Rep. Jared Polis, who contributed significant support throughout the research and publications process. We, of course, thank the members of the task force for lending their time, thoughtfulness, and extensive expertise on trade and development issues.

Over the course of the project, the project directors and authors were ably supported by CSIS staff, including Nahmyo Thomas and Paul Nadeau, as well as interns Michael Jacobs, Julia Marvin, and Elena Rosenblum. All contributed in some way to this report, either through research or logistical support. Finally, we are appreciative of the efforts of James Dunton, CSIS's head of publications.

CSIS Task Force on Trade Capacity Building

Cochairs

Representative Charles W. Boustany Jr., M.D. (R-LA)
Representative Jared S. Polis (D-CO)

Project Directors

Scott Miller
Senior Adviser and Scholl Chair in International Business, CSIS

Daniel F. Runde
William A. Schreyer Chair in Global Analysis and Director, Project on U.S. Leadership in Development, CSIS

Task Force Members

Thelma Askey
President, The Rockardt Group Global Strategies, and former Director, U.S. Trade and Development Agency

Tony Carroll
Senior Associate, Africa Program, CSIS

Paul H. DeLaney III
Partner, Kyle House Group, and former International Trade Counsel, U.S. Senate Committee on Finance

Andrea Durkin
Principal, Sparkplug, LLC

Erin M. Endean
Vice President, CARANA Corporation

Ana Guevara
President, AVENTI Associates, and former Alternate Executive Director for the United States, World Bank

Rod Hunter
Senior Vice President, International Affairs, PhRMA, and former Senior Director, National Security Council

Jeri Jensen
Principal, Business Driven Development, LLC

Katrin A. Kuhlmann
President and Founder, New Markets Lab

Kenneth A. Lanza
Senior Associate, CSIS

Michael A. Levett
Senior Associate, CSIS

Johanna Nesseth Tuttle
Manager, Development & Public Policy, Chevron

James Wallar
Senior Adviser, Nathan Associates

| A Letter from the Cochairs

Since the 1980s, the United States has provided trade capacity building (TCB) assistance to help developing countries participate in and benefit from global trade. Development policy and TCB have become increasingly interlinked as the global marketplace has grown and nations have become more economically interconnected. Regardless of ideology, there is agreement that improvements can be made in the TCB arena to create a level playing field for trade globally and within developing countries, so that nations can maximize the widest benefits from trade agreements, recognizing that efficiency, accountability, and transparency are critical. Through discussions with experts who have been on the front lines of implementing TCB in the past, we hope to provide a spotlight for areas where efficiencies can be improved and energy streamlined. This report aims at setting an improved and realistic framework for the administration and Congress to collaborate as the United States negotiates two trade agreements that are among the largest and have the most impact in U.S. history.

TCB is defined as assistance to help countries negotiate and implement trade agreements. It includes reforms to build the physical, human, and institutional capacity to benefit from trade and investment opportunities, including transparent regulatory and tax regimes to ensure a level playing field for entrepreneurs and other businesses. The United States is currently negotiating the Trans-Pacific Partnership (TPP) among 12 countries in the fast-growing region in the world representing nearly 40 percent of global GDP, as well as the Transatlantic Trade and Investment Partnership (T-TIP) where the combined GDP of the United States and European Union represents nearly 50 percent of world GDP. It is apparent that the world wants to engage in global trade as it creates jobs, investment and development opportunities, and allows for economic stability. However, as our world grows smaller with each new signed trade agreement, the task force believes that without the inclusion of TCB, we are limiting ourselves as to what is achievable through trade policy. It is through TCB that we can maximize the benefit provided by trade liberalization, as it ensures that our partner countries can meet the requirements of an agreement, but also ensures that the developing nation can capitalize on a new and beneficial trade agreement.

TCB unfortunately has not received the attention it deserves. The CSIS Bipartisan Congressional Task Force on Trade Capacity Building was created to highlight the critical role TCB can and should play in the U.S. trade agenda moving forward. Government and private-sector engagement has long been controversial and complicated in the realm of trade; however, we believe that the private sector can provide insight into which challenges, interests, and strategies should be addressed in specific nations. By engaging stakeholders who are established in country, aware of sensitivities, and who have already overcome obstacles, we will streamline the process for others as trade relations improve.

This paper offers a comprehensive look at existing problems through the perspectives of people who have stood in a developing nation and helped them to realize the economic and social benefits to trade. Specifically, this paper analyzes where TCB projects and partners can be found, and how to best use those existing resources to plan and implement selected TCB initiatives. We also strongly suggest that policy coordination between administrative structures could streamline TCB and ensure that methodology matches outlined goals.

It cannot be overstated that TCB is a vital piece of trade agreements and the success of those agreements moving forward in the twenty-first century. It is a case about trade, the benefits global trade can have on both the developed and developing world, and the returns of those efforts instead of focusing on the aid that can be offered. We can best achieve these aspirations by using the knowledge, resources, and skills already available from the private and federal workforce who have observed and witnessed firsthand the need for change. We have the tools to get the work done; we now must make the effort to see it through. Trade is an excellent way to create jobs, allow for economic stability, and improve relationships across the globe. Trade capacity building is a critical part of that equation.

Representative Charles W. Boustany Jr., M.D. (R-LA)
Representative Jared S. Polis (D-CO)

| Executive Summary

While free trade agreements and other intermediary trade agreements allow emerging nations increased access to global markets, many low- and middle-income countries lack the capacity to meet global standards. Deficiencies in quality of product, speed of transport, or quality of regulation can prevent countries from reaping the benefits of trade agreements, particularly with the United States.

Delivering benefits from new and sometimes controversial trade arrangements is crucial not only for developing countries, but for the United States as well. A global system of free trade and commerce that engages and allows for all to benefit, particularly developing country partners, should be viewed in the context of the broader U.S. national interest. In order to demonstrate the importance of trade capacity building (TCB), it is critical to highlight its value from the U.S. perspective, in addition to its value to partner countries. TCB serves the interests of the United States on a number of fronts, including: promoting development and economic growth in order to further regional and global stability and security; supporting and elaborating a rules-based trading system that encourages economic stability; and easing access to markets and facilitating supply chains that strengthen commercial interests. This paper highlights these interests, addresses outstanding questions, and fills in knowledge gaps in the U.S. government's TCB methodology.

TCB has long existed as a pillar of American development assistance, delivered principally by the U.S. Agency for International Development (USAID) and its private partners, but TCB has rarely been comprehensively examined or planned like many other key sectors. This paper aims to distill lessons from past TCB efforts and build a practical agenda for improving future planning, coordination, and implementation.

The paper focuses on how TCB projects can be best planned and coordinated more efficiently in order to leverage expertise and tools across agencies.

In order to improve the U.S. government's ability to deliver TCB assistance:

- The president should form a permanent interagency committee to improve whole-of-government coordination on TCB assistance. The committee should be composed of representatives drawn from the core U.S. government agencies relevant to TCB efforts, and leadership of the committee should be granted based on convening power and relevance to the TCB process.

- The interagency committee should:

  o Agree upon a succinct and clear definition of TCB assistance.

○ Create a set of strategic criteria used to select developing country partners that would most benefit from TCB support. By establishing a selection framework the committee provides itself a clearly bound agenda, and mitigates the risk of regional priorities absorbing TCB funds without solid rationale. It will be critical to apply these criteria to identify 10 to 15 countries that can benefit from TCB, while also ensuring the presence of sufficient political will to effectively implement stated reforms.

- Congress should create a line item in the Foreign Operations budget for TCB activities. This would not require new appropriations, and instead could be achieved by consolidating existing TCB dollars currently scattered across various U.S. agencies and accounts. This money would be allocated at the discretion of the interagency coordination committee.

- At the country level, the U.S. ambassador should be designated as the local coordinator for U.S. government-led TCB activity. He or she would work in concert with the USAID mission director, the U.S. Foreign Commercial Service, and the interagency committee to identify reform opportunities and apply TCB resources.

- The U.S. ambassador should convene an ad hoc advisory committee, coordinated by the U.S. Commercial Service, composed primarily of private-sector representatives, both local and multinational, that are currently doing business in the country being targeted for trade capacity building. These representatives would provide local context and expertise, and could advise on where TCB efforts and resources can be best expended.

1 | Introduction

What Is Trade Capacity Building?

Trade capacity building (TCB) refers to development assistance that aims to increase a country's ability to engage in global trade. This can be technical assistance, training, or other financial support that will strengthen the inherent capacity of a country to trade goods and services on the global market, but also includes measures to assist in the production of goods for export. Since TCB most often refers to all aspects of trade development assistance (capacity building, technical assistance in regulatory agreements, physical infrastructure, and job training, among many others) there are many ways in which government agencies, nongovernmental organizations (NGOs), and private-sector donors participate in TCB efforts. While most organizations define the term broadly, a more focused definition of TCB activities would help improve the effectiveness of monitoring and evaluation efforts, as well as to better identify what is spent on TCB each year and the impact of those dollars.

According to the U.S. Agency for International Development's (USAID) Trade Capacity Building Database, which uses a broad definition of TCB, the United States is one of the leading TCB providers in the world, contributing $712 million in total support in 2013, and a total of $15.9 billion from 2000 to 2013, aiding activities in 125 countries and territories.[1] TCB assistance is provided by the United States to developing economies in a variety of ways through various agencies. The most widely known TCB funder is USAID,[2] but the Millennium Challenge Corporation (MCC) has been a close second since 2005, and was in fact the largest single funder in 2008, providing over $1.6 billion in funding for TCB-related activities.[3] Though, as the chart in section 2 suggests, MCC funding is also the cause of large fluctuation in TCB spending levels in recent years. While USAID and MCC have been the primary sources of funding, there are more than 20 other federal agencies and departments that contribute to this effort. This makes coordinating TCB assistance a significant challenge, and more cohesive planning of projects has the potential to increase the efficiency of TCB programming overall.

---

[1] U.S. Agency for International Development (USAID), "USAID Trade Capacity Building Database," http://tcb.eads.usaidallnet.gov.
[2] Molly Hageboeck et al., *From Aid to Trade: Delivering Results. A Cross-Country Evaluation of USAID Trade Capacity Building* (Washington, DC: USAID, November 2010), http://pdf.usaid.gov/pdf_docs/PDACR202.pdf. According to this report, from 1999 to 2009 USAID provided roughly $5 billion in TCB aid, some 42 percent of total TCB funding.
[3] U.S. Agency for International Development (USAID), "USAID Trade Capacity Building Database," http://tcb.eads.usaidallnet.gov.

Economic development policy and TCB have become increasingly interlinked as the global market place has grown and nations have become more economically interconnected. Requests from developing country negotiating partners for capacity building assistance are increasingly common and, because greater trade capacity promises self-reliance and economic growth, are increasingly valuable to developing countries. In addition, TCB can be a useful lever for the United States to secure commitments from partner countries in negotiating agreements. This is particularly true given the recognition that TCB provides an infusion of private-sector disciplines, including transfer of knowledge, technology, and experience that many countries are eager to gain.

Modern trade agreements with low- and middle-income countries typically include provisions to build trade capacity in order to maximize the benefits provided by trade liberalization. This is vital for developing countries, as they often lack the human and institutional capacity to take advantage of the potential of a new trade agreement. For the United States, TCB helps secure and implement additional liberalization in negotiations, but also ensures that the partner country has the capability to meet the requirements of the agreement. From both perspectives, TCB is a crucial tool for securing and capitalizing upon new and beneficial trade agreements.

Increasingly, the trade and development nexus represents the area in which donors and partner countries can support maximum economic growth and development impact. Trade now encompasses diverse economic and political engagements across international borders, and provides a unique vehicle to encourage comprehensive reforms in arenas from business regulation to physical infrastructure. As the composition of international trade diversifies and the direction of trade flows becomes more complex, the methodologies and structures that facilitate trade must undergo an accompanying shift.

Trade has become more relevant as a developmental tool against the backdrop of unsteady, and in many cases declining, Official Development Assistance (ODA). ODA from the Development Assistance Committee (DAC) of the Organization for Economic Cooperation and Development (OECD) has declined as a percentage of gross national income (GNI) each year since 2010. Flows from the United States, the world's largest single donor, have remained largely stagnant over this period.[4] Further, wealthy nations are less willing to continue longstanding one-way preference systems, even for least-developed countries, reflecting the challenging fiscal situation faced by traditional OECD bilateral donors, but also the outstanding economic progress made by much of the developing world in recent decades. Trade offers a mutually beneficial

---

[4] Organization for Economic Cooperation and Development (OECD), "Statistics on Resource Flows to Developing Countries: Table 8—ODA by Individual DAC Countries at 2012 Prices and Exchange Rates," http://www.oecd.org/development/stats/statisticsonresourceflowstodevelopingcountries.htm.

channel for supporting development outcomes without relying upon either costly ODA or paternalistic preference programs.

TCB is more necessary than ever, as trade is increasingly comprehensive and complex; from negotiation through to implementation, modern trade agreements require engagement that is both broader and deeper than in previous generations. Trade and investment agreements encompass an expanding range of nontariff, regulatory, and investment barriers that impact the ability of developing countries to participate in regional and global supply and value chains. In this sense, the countries that stand to gain the most from increased international economic engagement are often ill equipped to capture the benefits of trade. Trade agreements and World Trade Organization (WTO) obligations are complex, and require a great deal of institutional and regulatory capacity, as well as business acumen. Articles addressing sanitary and phytosanitary (SPS) measures, trade-related aspects of intellectual property rights (TRIPS), complex trade in services, customs modernization, and technical barriers to trade (TBT) are now standard inclusions in trade agreements. On the domestic front, developing countries already face challenges in explaining to constituents the benefits of the trade agreements they have negotiated. On top of this challenge, they are often underequipped as negotiators and subsequently lack the ability to meet the stipulated obligations due to a lack of interagency coordination and political commitment to fully implementing these obligations. This arrangement can be harmful for countries that are unable to capture the benefits of trade and investment, as well as for the United States as it seeks beneficial economic ties and opportunities for U.S. companies to expand in emerging markets.

The last two decades brought growing recognition of the challenge of implementing trade agreements, and an accompanying increase in attention for TCB efforts. The 1994 Uruguay Round significantly increased the number of contracting parties, as well as the types of economic activity that fell under its auspice.[5] This expansion was accompanied by recognition on the part of the WTO that "developing country members have undertaken significant new commitments, both substantive and procedural," as well as assurance that there would be "an integrated approach to assisting these countries in enhancing their trading opportunities."[6] Despite this commitment, the WTO stalled on the issue, but did lay out a framework that was later borrowed by the United States in bilateral agreements. TCB efforts began in earnest in several U.S.-led trade agreements, first in the Dominican Republic–Central America–United States Free Trade Agreement (CAFTA-DR) and then in agreements with

---

[5] Eric T. Miller, *Achievements and Challenges of Trade Capacity Building: A Practitioner's Analysis of the CAFTA Process and Its Lessons for the Multilateral System* (Buenos Aires: Institute for the Integration of Latin America and the Caribbean, October 2005), 6, http://idbdocs.iadb.org/wsdocs/ getdocument.aspx?docnum=33006102.
[6] World Trade Organization (WTO), "Singapore WTO Ministerial Declaration: Adopted on 13 December 1996," paragraphs 10 and 11, http://www.wto.org/english/thewto_e/minist_e/min96_e/wtodec_e.htm.

Colombia, Panama, and Peru. TCB is now considered a standard component of U.S. trade agreements with developing countries.

After 10 years of U.S. experience with TCB in trade agreements, there is an opportunity to consolidate and capitalize on lessons learned. Though a number of TCB initiatives have brought success, the United States would benefit greatly from an in-depth analysis of best practices and improved interagency coordination to establish a replicable and sustainable methodology. There are substantial economic benefits to be unlocked for both the United States and recipient nations. Furthermore, TCB functions as a catalyst for structural economic reform and good governance, as it provides the incentive and resources for trade and investment liberalization. In the coming years, there will be several high-profile opportunities to use a revamped TCB approach. The Trans-Pacific Partnership (TPP), currently under negotiation with the United States and 11 other countries, provides a vehicle for combining best practices from leading global TCB implementers, as well as the opportunity to divide the cost. In this regard, TPP could set a new global standard on TCB, which could lead to a more connected, prosperous, and stable world.

TCB in the U.S. Context

In the 1980s the United States began providing trade capacity-related assistance to its neighbors through the Caribbean Basin Initiative (CBI), but did so without any official mention of TCB. Still, U.S. development programming began incorporating TCB with the CBI, which served as part of a larger geostrategic plan in the region. Following an announcement by President Ronald Reagan on February 24, 1982, the United States began providing a mix of tax incentives and trade preferences for select countries in Latin America and the Caribbean.[7] In 1990, the Caribbean Basin Economic Recovery Expansion Act, known as CBI 2, made the preferences permanent.[8] Criticism of the CBI program centered on implementation and design; there were limited trade gains and they were focused primarily in the textile and resource industries.[9] Further complaints were drawn by the perceived paternalistic nature of trade preference programs, which critics argue are one-sided concessions determined and offered unilaterally by the donor nation.

The CBI effort still served as a useful precursor for TCB in the negotiation process for the Free Trade Area of the Americas (FTAA), and more importantly, CAFTA-DR, leading to a string of American bilateral trade agreements that included TCB

---

[7] Ronald Reagan, "Remarks on the Caribbean Basin Initiative to the Permanent Council of the Organization of American States" (speech, Organization of American States, Washington, D.C., February 24, 1982), http://www.presidency.ucsb.edu/ws/?pid=42202.

[8] Caribbean Basin Economic Recovery Expansion Act of 1990, Pub. L. 101-382, title II, Aug. 20, 1990, http://www.law.cornell.edu/topn/caribbean_basin_economic_recovery_expansion_act_of_1990.

[9] J. F. Hornbeck, *U.S. Trade Policy and the Caribbean: From Trade Preferences to Free Trade Agreements* (Washington, DC: Congressional Research Service, January 6, 2011), 5, http://www.fas.org/sgp/crs/row/RL33951.pdf.

provisions. The experience in CBI was used to construct a methodological framework for TCB during negotiation of FTAA. In 2001 FTAA ministers of trade established a Hemispheric Cooperation Program (HCP), which was responsible for technical assistance and training for trade negotiation and implementation processes.[10] The next year, the ministers of trade laid down explicit language charging the HCP with providing financial and nonfinancial assistance for countries seeking to build trade capacity.

With greater clarification regarding the support it would be required to provide, the HCP approached the Inter-American Development Bank and the Multilateral Investment Fund (MIF) regarding specific strategies for implementing capacity-building assistance. Progress on the FTAA eventually froze, but it provided a broad framework for TCB assistance in the Western Hemisphere.

---

[10] Miller, *Achievements and Challenges of Trade Capacity Building*, 15.

2 | Current TCB Landscape and Challenges

Centralized Trade Policy and Decentralized Aid

Greater policy coordination between administrative structures could streamline TCB efforts and ensure that methodology matches the outlined goals. Currently USAID, MCC, the U.S. Trade Representative (USTR), the U.S. Trade and Development Agency (USTDA), the U.S. Commercial Service, the U.S. Agricultural Service, and 14 other U.S. agencies are all engaged in TCB in one form or another. Through the trade advisory committee system, the private sector also has a mechanism for involvement—but these committees are focused on trade negotiation and agreement provisions rather than how to operationally build capacity to meet trade commitments. Difficulty arises because separate organizations are given preeminence in the distinct phases of the process, inhibiting a smooth and integrated strategy and implementation.

For example, while USTR holds the right to negotiate trade agreements on behalf of the president, including TCB chapters, the private sector is often best positioned to know what TCB projects would be most beneficial in a given country. Similarly, USTR expects that USAID or MCC will implement TCB projects, but does not consult with the organizations in project selection or design. Moreover, a lack of an interagency TCB strategy that sets priorities, identifies best practices, and develops common measurements of success hampers a whole-of-government approach to TCB. The myriad agencies engaged in various TCB efforts around the world also complicates and interferes with the ability of U.S. businesses to engage with the U.S. government in an efficient way to share its operational expertise and recommendations to inform the design and implementation of TCB funding.

The development implementation community tends to prefer self-directed policy rather than centralized policy from Washington. Similarly, USTR tends to view input from the aid world as interfering with its prerogative as chief representative and negotiator for U.S. trade interests. USAID may "know best" in terms of development issues, but undervalues the need to coordinate with central goals and policy disseminated by the administration. USTR often underestimates or miscalculates the relevance and challenges associated with specific development projects. U.S. Commercial Service officers, who often clearly see the needs of the U.S. and local private sectors in given markets, are unable to provide assistance given their current congressional mandate of focusing on exports. Private-sector actors pursue TCB activities most relevant to individual industries and business practices, not always considering how they fit into the broader operation and strategic goals of trade programs. Trade is a strong modern development vehicle in that it serves as a nexus for various communities and organizations, but it demands a high degree of coordination and mutual understanding between these players to achieve stated goals, and more broadly, economic growth. Institutional disconnects and interagency stove-piped decisionmaking, ongoing skepticism between business and the development community leaders, and the failure to align TCB programs with the economic and market opportunities and challenges in specific developing countries dilute and undermine the effectiveness of TCB efforts by the U.S. government and constrain the ability of developing countries to realize the full benefits that expanded trade and investment can ignite.

USAID and MCC Have Provided the Vast Majority of Funding since 2005

While more than 20 federal agencies and departments contribute money to TCB, the vast majority of TCB funding since 2005 has come from USAID and the Millennium Challenge Corporation (MCC). From 2000 to 2013, USAID provided roughly $6.9 billion in TCB aid, accounting for more than 40 percent of total U.S. TCB funding; since 2005, MCC has also become a significant player in TCB. It is important to note that MCC funding was highest from 2005 to 2012, with significantly lower funding both before and after, but MCC still accounts for 33 percent of U.S. TCB funding since 2000.[11] The chart below shows U.S. TCB funding by source.[12]

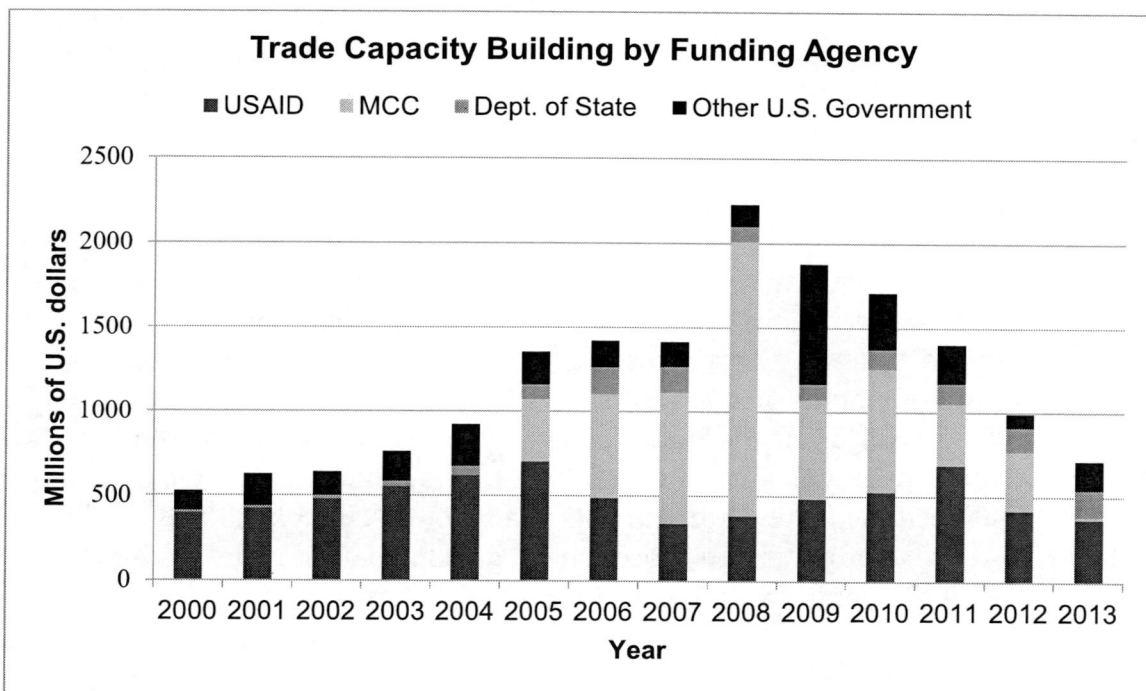

Trade Capacity Building by Funding Agency
■ USAID ▦ MCC ▦ Dept. of State ■ Other U.S. Government

---

[11] Hageboeck et al., *From Aid to Trade.*
[12] USAID, "USAID Trade Capacity Building Database."

Despite being the most prominent and often most effective U.S. aid implementers, particularly in regards to TCB, neither USAID nor MCC is sufficiently engaged in TCB goal identification. The trade advisory boards do not generally include USAID or MCC representation, and are directed by USTR, which holds an agenda distinct and separate from either of the major aid-implementing agencies. In most cases, implementation of TCB projects will fall to either USAID or MCC but neither organization coordinates with USTR.

USAID and MCC must be integrated into forming TCB goals; this integration would serve to more effectively inform the selection of goals, but would also allow the organizations to plan for TCB fund allocation more efficiently. In both organizations, budgets tend to be inflexible and are planned long before implementation. USTR cannot inform USAID and MCC of areas that require TCB effort, and expect a quick reallocation of funds. Incorporating USAID and MCC into the early stages of TCB goal formation would be beneficial, but a flexible spending account or specific budget line item for TCB to be allocated across various organizations would be even more useful. As it stands, the organizations being asked to implement TCB projects are not given sufficient voice in the process nor the flexibility to best carry out these programs.

USAID and MCC must also better integrate the operational expertise and priorities of the business community and other stakeholders that actually conduct business, trade, and run development assistance programs within developing countries who receive TCB funding. Failure to integrate private-sector and stakeholder recommendations at the beginning of any TCB efforts, programming, or resource allocations can severely limit the economic impact of these programs and result in disconnects between how the TCB funding is allocated and the commercial realities on the ground in the recipient countries.

Interagency Coordination

Creating an interagency committee with a coordinator to serve as chairperson of the committee for all TCB-related activity would help cut down on redundancies and increase collaboration among all actors. Ideally USTR would not be given control of this position, as it already holds primacy in trade-related issues, and is primarily focused on negotiation. USAID or the State Department would likely supply this person given their critical involvement in TCB, but State is uniquely suited to the role as it sits at the intersection of trade, foreign policy, aid, and security. The TCB coordinator would consider the entire process from goal formation in the lead-up to negotiations through the implementation and evaluation phases.

While creating a TCB coordinator provides an attractive hypothetical solution to the challenge of multiple agencies, there are practical hurdles associated with creating this position. Specifically, the effectiveness of the individual would be determined by the level of knowledge and influence wielded by the person placed in this role. An effective leader would require both convening authority and substantive knowledge and trade and development issues.

The United States has already recognized the need for coordination on TCB issues, but the responses thus far are too limited in authority and scope. For example, the president formed a Steering Group on Africa Trade and Investment Capacity Building in August 2014, but it is unclear whether the group will provide recommendations only or if they wield independent decisionmaking power.[13] The group is also focused exclusively on Africa, which is a priority region, but interagency coordination on TCB assistance would be relevant in countries and regions around the world. The United States did create a TCB interagency group cochaired by USAID and USTR in 2002,[14] but it was unclear what authority and role this group held, and it has since dissolved.

Incorporate U.S. Customs and Border Protection into the TCB Process

In the post–9/11 era, trade and security are closely related. As goods, services, and people flow from one country to another, there are clear security implications. Accordingly, there are trade-related antiterror security measures that dictate what may enter the United States, as well as the specific process of entry. While there is a clear impetus and need for these measures, overly onerous security requirements have the potential to impact developing economies' prospects for profitable trade with the United States. Trade, development, and security are intimately linked, and incorporating U.S. Customs and Border Protection into the TCB process would be a key step in creating a more integrated and comprehensive strategy on all of these fronts. U.S. Customs and Border Protection has undergone a transformation over the past five years in an effort to develop best practices that improve security and enhance trade enforcement, while also facilitating and expediting the movement of legitimate goods. The creation of Centers of Excellence and Expertise, the negotiation of mutual recognition agreements, and improvements to U.S. trusted trader programs all improve U.S. trade competitiveness, and these reforms and CBP's expertise are critical to encouraging and providing technical assistance to developing country customs authorities to share best practices so they can expand trade as well.

As it stands, security measures and customs requirements, as well as developing countries' ability to meet these requirements, limit trade and development. Currently,

---

[13] The White House, "Presidential Memorandum—Establishing a Comprehensive Approach to Expanding Sub-Saharan Africa's Capacity for Trade and Investment," August 4, 2014, http://www.whitehouse.gov/the-press-office/2014/08/04/presidential-memorandum-establishing-comprehensive-approach-expanding-su.
[14] U.S. Government Accountability Office (GAO), *Foreign Assistance: U.S. Trade Capacity Building Extensive, but Its Effectiveness Has Yet to Be Evaluated*, Report to Congressional Requesters, GAO-05-150 (Washington, DC: GAO, February 2005), http://www.gao.gov/assets/250/245277.pdf.

U.S. Customs and Border Protection's Container Security Initiative (CSI, which pre-screens roughly 80 percent of all containerized cargo destined for the United States at 58 ports worldwide) operates in only two ports in Africa: Alexandria, Egypt, and Durban, South Africa.[15] Other ports in Africa that are not participating in CSI do not receive the benefits of working closely with a U.S. Customs and Border Protection team yet may still face the same hurdles posed by stringent container-security measures should their cargo be destined for the United States. While the United States should not relax these measures, there is an opportunity to coordinate and streamline requirements as well as assist developing country partners in meeting their customs and border security obligations.

By involving Customs and Border Protection in TCB, both the United States and developing country partners can establish a clear understanding of specific security shortcomings and ways to address these weak points at the earliest stages of trade negotiation. Typically, developing country partners are expected to finance their own security, and only then can they gain the benefits of U.S. trade. The reality, however, is that reaching compliance is both costly and time consuming. U.S. assistance can help developing country partners identify and strengthen their risk management.

While Customs and Border Protection has traditionally functioned as an enforcement agency, the organization is increasingly charged with streamlining border processes. As Customs and Border Protection is more engaged in facilitating trade, measures including electronic "single window" (all data submitted in one data field and simultaneously transmitted to all relevant agencies) are now priorities. U.S. government agencies have been hesitant to take up "single window" and other trade-facilitation measures, prompting the White House to issue an Executive Order requiring a single window to be set up and, important for this paper, to "encourage other countries to develop similar single window systems to facilitate the sharing of relevant data, as appropriate, across governmental systems and with trading partners."[16] That exchange of information can be used to assess and pre-clear shipments and also strengthen security—the future of trade. In sum, Customs and Border Protection should be involved to help coordinate TCB for countries to build the institutional and professional capacity for electronic information systems that can facilitate the cross-border processing of goods as well as to facilitate the exchange of information to strengthen security of shipments to and from the United States.

---

[15] U.S. Customs and Border Protection, "CSI: Container Security Initiative," http://www.cbp.gov/border-security/ports-entry/cargo-security/csi/csi-brief.
[16] Barack Obama, "Executive Order—Streamlining the Export/Import Process for America's Businesses," White House, February 19, 2014, http://www.whitehouse.gov/the-press-office/2014/02/19/executive-order-streamlining-exportimport-process-america-s-businesses.

Focus on In-Country Planning Rather Than Remote Direction from Washington, D.C.

While there are clear imperatives for maintaining some central coordination and oversight of overall TCB efforts, there must be greater prominence for actors and strategies that originate on the ground in developing partner countries. While USTR is a Washington-centric organization focused on broader negotiating priorities, it would benefit from contextually specific understanding and insight in formulating and implementing TCB that could come from consultations with representatives from implementing agencies with country-specific knowledge. Fortunately, the United States has several options in terms of human resources capable of providing this type of information, including:

- The U.S. ambassador

- USAID country mission director and staff

- Foreign Agricultural Service Officers

- Foreign Service Economic Officers

- Foreign Commercial Service Officers

- Private-sector country managers

All of these actors are capable of providing nuanced and relevant analysis of the economic, political, and business conditions in the countries in which they operate. Identifying and mobilizing these actors so that they are integrated in TCB efforts from formulation through implementation will be critical in constructing country-specific TCB methodologies. Development of country-specific TCB plans drawing on the expertise in the mission of the full range of agencies and incorporating the experience of the U.S. private sector on the ground in each country will provide a strategic framework to prioritize TCB funding and programming in each country and can be shaped by broader policy priorities identified in Washington, D.C.

It will subsequently be crucial that these actors have the ability to connect back with those charged with formulating central policy in Washington, D.C. The U.S. ambassador would likely be well positioned to serve in this role, and it should be noted that the ambassador has a critical role coordinating and pushing action in partner countries, but there should be a formalized mechanism for this communication and consultation to occur.

Identify Partners Capable of Mobilizing Resources and Reform

While it's relatively straightforward to identify points of weakness in trade capacity, it is difficult to identify effective partners and approaches for addressing these shortcomings. Aside from the practical challenge of addressing gaps in trade capacity, there is the further difficulty of untangling the interests, incentives, and institutions that led to the existing arrangement. Any efforts to shift such an arrangement must incorporate both technical solutions and tactical approaches.

Following the conclusion of a trade agreement, or the identification of a high-priority TCB objective from the U.S. point of view, the host-country government should be solicited for a list of its own TCB and development priorities. The U.S. interagency committee should identify the host priorities that align with our own, and then solicit project development from U.S. agencies to address these priorities. The United States and host country should identify private-sector and NGO expertise, advice, and participation as needed. Finally, the United States should then select and further develop those TCB projects that will address the joint priorities identified in the process. This is particularly relevant in countries where small groups of political and economic elites capture the majority of benefits and income associated with trade flows. There is little motivation for these elites to alter the existing arrangement, even if doing so is associated with broad economic growth and benefit. Under the correct conditions, trade serves to level the economic playing field. Unfortunately, in certain contexts trade can drive further inequality.

Successful TCB clearly requires significant, contextually specific knowledge and experience, but also careful project selection. Some environments are not suitable for TCB assistance and developing a framework or criteria to identify where we should and should not pursue TCB would be a valuable asset. Clear selection criteria would also serve as a hand-tying exercise, and would prevent short-term priorities from dictating project selection. To make an informed assessment evaluating the capacity of each country to benefit from TCB programs and funding requires coordination and consultation with the private sector that conducts trade in each country. Even if a country passes laws and issues regulations that meet trade commitments, the enforcement and political will to follow through on these policies can be best determined by working closely with the businesses and stakeholders in country that actually trade and invest there.

Key Opportunities for TCB

Looking ahead, there are opportunities to use TCB in upcoming U.S. trade agreements, but also outside of the context of official trade agreements. The largest existing item in the U.S. trade docket is the Trans-Pacific Partnership (TPP). TPP aims to engage 11 countries along the Pacific Rim in the agreement, and would include a mix of developing and developed countries.[17] Given the diverse economies involved, TPP would benefit from a TCB provision that enabled all parties to capture the full range of benefits offered by the trade agreement. Developing countries will need assistance meeting obligations and building systems to more smoothly integrate the new trade and investment opportunities in the regional trade agreement, and developed countries have the opportunity to leverage and coordinate TCB resources to maximize participation and benefits across TPP countries. TPP draws together donor countries well versed in TCB practice, and with large corresponding aid budgets. There is a window for a well-funded TCB program based on best practices that sets a new global standard moving forward.

The WTO Trade Facilitation Agreement (TFA) provides a more immediate TCB opportunity. WTO members formally adopted the TFA on November 27, 2014; this is the first multilateral agreement in the 20-year history of the WTO and is now open to ratification by WTO members. To date, 50 developing countries have notified their Category A commitments and upon ratification will identify the TFA commitments for which they need additional TCB support.[18] The second round of commitments will be those that require technical assistance—for example, TCB, with the U.S. government prepared to offer assistance to developing countries that demonstrate the political will to adopt the highest standards and best practices in implementing the TFA commitments and that are significant U.S. trading partners.

The adoption of the TFA sets a road map of trade-facilitation reforms each WTO member must adopt, while also setting in place a process for developing countries to identify TCB needs, with the developed country and donor community providing funding to meet those needs. To realize the full potential of free trade agreements and the WTO TFA requires the U.S. government to reset and prioritize its trade-capacity programs to maximize the positive impact these programs and funds can play to stimulate trade and investment. Moreover, U.S. TCB strategies must better align and coordinate with other developed-country trade capacity efforts as well as the multilateral and regional development banks and international financial organizations to share best practices and leverage limited resources.

A regional approach to TCB, which has merit from both an organizational and a practical point of view,[19] might be a logical way to begin this process and best promote the adoption of best practices. Each major region has its trade groups, and U.S.-led TCB could help strengthen these groups while promoting their consistency with WTO

---

[17] Office of the U.S. Trade Representative, "Trans-Pacific Partnership (TPP): Unlocking Opportunity for Americans through Trade with the Asia Pacific," https://ustr.gov/tpp.

[18] World Trade Organization (WTO), "Trade facilitation," http://www.wto.org/english/tratop_e/tradfa_e/tradfa_e.htm.

[19] OECD, *The Development Dimension: Regional Perspectives on Aid for Trade* (Paris: OECD, November 2014).

rules. Thus, TPP, Asia-Pacific Economic Cooperation (APEC), U.S.-Association of Southeast Asian Nations (ASEAN) Expanded Economic Engagement, African Growth and Opportunity Act (AGOA), and other regional initiatives could serve as starting points for TCB-linked assistance. Moreover, actively engaging with the private sector and businesses that trade in these WTO developing country members to identify gaps and fund best practices will be critical to achieving the full trade benefits envisioned in adopting the TFA.

3 | TCB Case Studies

Case: TCB in CAFTA-DR

The Dominican Republic–Central America–United States Free Trade Agreement (CAFTA-DR) includes a chapter on TCB that states that the parties recognize "that trade capacity building assistance is a catalyst for the reforms and investments necessary to foster trade-driven economic growth, poverty reduction, and adjustment to liberalized trade," and that "the Parties hereby establish a Committee on Trade Capacity Building, comprising representatives of each Party." This TCB committee was the first of its kind for any free trade agreement. It was tasked with prioritizing TCB projects at the national or regional level, inviting appropriate international donor institutions, private-sector entities, and NGOs to assist in implementing TCB projects, working with other committees or working groups in the agreement in support of TCB projects, monitoring and assessing progress in implementing TCB projects, and reporting annually to the commission describing the TCB committee's activities. Finally, the parties established an initial working group on customs and trade facilitation that was to report to the TCB committee. The CAFTA-DR was signed by President George W. Bush on July 28, 2005, and first entered into force in El Salvador, Honduras, Nicaragua, and Guatemala by July 1, 2006, followed by the Dominican Republic on March 1, 2007, and Costa Rica on January 1, 2009.

CAFTA-DR's effects on overall bilateral trade have been significant: U.S. imports from the six CAFTA-DR countries were around $18 billion in 2005, the year before CAFTA-DR came into force. That number increased almost 68 percent to $30.1 billion in 2013. U.S. exports to the CAFTA-DR countries stood at about $16.9 billion in 2005, but increased by 75 percent to $29.5 billion in 2013. CAFTA-DR had an overwhelmingly positive influence on total trade between the United States and CAFTA-DR countries.

Between 2003 and July 2007, the U.S. government provided more than $659 million in trade-related assistance to the CAFTA-DR countries. This assistance came from USAID, the Overseas Private Investment Corporation (OPIC), the U.S. Trade and Development Agency, the Millennium Challenge Corporation, and the U.S. Departments of Agriculture, State, Commerce, Treasury, and Homeland Security. Some of the activities funded by this TCB assistance included general trade infrastructure improvements like port modernization, microfinancing aimed at small businesses, and assistance to small farmers in the form of new irrigation systems and other infrastructure improvements. For example, USAID's Rural Economic Diversification Program (RED) taught plantain producers in Honduras high-density planting and other advanced agricultural techniques like drip irrigation and disease controls that would help prepare their crops for international markets. As a result of RED assistance, USAID-assisted farmers in the agriculturally focused Yoro region of Honduras were able to increase plantain sales from 2 million pounds in 2005 to 7 million pounds in 2008. Similar TCB success stories played a major role in helping farmers and other groups threatened by the CAFTA-DR to navigate the changes they faced as the agreement came into force, and similar programs were established as part of subsequent trade agreements with other Latin American countries.

As a result of CAFTA-DR's TCB provisions, as well as the learning process it provided, TCB efforts were mainstreamed into subsequent trade negotiating. Practical matters of coordination between donors and implementing countries were also improved, opening the door for TCB components in other U.S. trade agreements, including those with Peru, Colombia, and Panama.

Case: TCB in the Peru Trade Promotion Agreement

The Peru Trade Promotion Agreement (PTPA), signed on April 12, 2006, includes a chapter on TCB with nearly identical language to that of CAFTA. In it, the parties to the agreement recognize "that trade capacity building is a catalyst for the reforms and investments necessary to foster trade-driven economic growth, poverty reduction, and adjustment to liberalized trade." In keeping with that belief, the chapter established a TCB committee that was tasked with the following: updating the committee on the national TCB strategy; prioritizing those projects; working with international aid organizations, private enterprises, NGOs, government agencies, and other committees created by the agreement to develop and implement projects; monitoring and assessing projects; and reporting annually to the commission. The chapter also established an initial working group on customs administration and trade facilitation.

As part of the implementation of the PTPA, the TCB working group, made up of the Inter-American Development Bank, the World Bank, the Organization of American States, and the Economic Commission for Latin America and the Caribbean (ECLAC), called on the committee to address economic assistance issues including programs to aid small and medium-sized enterprises, rural farmers, food safety inspectors, and customs officials. Based on those recommendations, Peru developed programs with key stakeholders to address these issues, including training and assistance in trade facilitation, intellectual property, business registration, labor, regulation of pharmaceuticals, and telecommunication. Over this period of development from 2004 to 2006, the U.S. government provided approximately $57 million in TCB assistance to Peru.[20] Peru has also benefited from multilateral lenders such as the Inter-American Development Bank and the World Bank.

---

[20] "USAID Trade Capacity Building Database," https://eads.usaid.gov/tcb/data/funding_detail.cfm?detailName=country_id&detailValue=604&tab=funding.

The PTPA overall was successful in fostering U.S. trade with Peru, with imports increasing from $5.9 billion in 2006 to $8.1 billion in 2013 and exports increasing from $2.9 billion to $10.1 billion. Furthermore, a 2014 report by the U.S. Department of Agriculture found that "exports of U.S. consumer-oriented products at a record $212 million now account for 25 percent of U.S. food exports to Peru."

Specific interventions in Peru included improving labor standards, reforming trade facilitation, streamlining business registration, and modernizing intellectual property rights. The United States worked with the Peruvian Ministry of Labor to better monitor labor standards and improve institutional capacity to manage labor disputes resulting in a 27 percent increase in labor inspection orders from 2009 to 2011, and the duration of labor disputes declined from 54 months in 2010 to 7 months in 2012; health and safety protocols were also standardized. As a result of the United States' support for a single window and training on pre-clearance, among other trade facilitation programs, the time to export declined from 22 to 12 days and the time to import declined from 29 to 17 days.

Additionally, there is evidence that TCB positively influences several indicators of growth in developing countries in general. A 2010 cross-country report by USAID found that "USAID TCB projects have a positive effect on developing country exports, even in very poor countries and those dealing with conflict within their borders. At the national level, the statistical association found by the evaluation between export gains and TCB assistance varies depending on the status of a number of critical external and domestic factors that are known to significantly influence developing country export performance." However, more research is needed to isolate the effect the TCB provisions of the PTPA had on Peru's economy on a larger scale.

Case: TCB in the Colombia Trade Promotion Agreement and Free Trade Agreement

Colombia initially received TCB support through the Andean regional project from 2004 to 2006. Though the program was short-lived, Colombia saw benefits in trade facilitation and intellectual property rights. The Colombia Trade Promotion Agreement, which came into effect on May 15, 2014, also includes a chapter on TCB with language nearly identical to that found in the PTPA and CAFTA-DR. As in the Peru case, the agreement calls for establishing a TCB committee that will prioritize TCB projects, invite "appropriate international donor institutions, private sector entities, and nongovernmental organizations" to assist in implementation of TCB projects, monitor and assess progress regarding implementation of TCB projects, and report annually to the commission on the committee's activities. Finally, as in the Peru and CAFTA-DR cases, the parties agreed to establish a working group on customs administration and trade facilitation that will report to the committee.

The Colombian government expected the CTPA to greatly increase exports for Colombia, with an increase of 10 percent in exports and an additional one percentage point of economic growth in 2012, creating 300,000 jobs. Although the CTPA's overall effects on the U.S. economy will be relatively small due to trade with Colombia making up only a small percentage of total U.S. trade (1 percent in 2013), some of the effects of the CTPA can already be observed domestically, as merchandise exports to Colombia in 2013 increased to $16.5 billion from $12.8 billion in 2011, an increase of 29 percent in just two years. While part of this increase in exports must be attributed to a recovery in trade following the 2008 financial crisis, the CTPA probably contributed to this development, though it is still too early to tell just how much is directly related to the CTPA. What we do know for sure is that trade between the United States and Colombia is on a positive trajectory following approval of the CTPA.

Finally, while it may be too early to see the direct effects of TCB in the context of the CTPA, it would be useful to identify specific industries that would most benefit from TCB support. For example, farmers in Colombia's poultry industry are threatened by poultry imports from America that will now cost half the price of that produced in Colombia. In order for Colombia's poultry farmers to benefit from CTPA, TCB efforts must be made either in the form of infrastructure improvements that could reduce transportation costs for the farmers, or through trade adjustment assistance in the form of labor-reeducation or small business development that would allow poultry farmers to move into other jobs or scale up their operations to better compete with foreign companies, thus minimizing the CTPA's harmful effects and maximizing its long-term benefits.

Case: TCB in the Panama Trade Promotion Agreement

The Panama Trade Promotion Agreement (PTPA), like the Peru TPA and Colombia TPA, also includes a chapter on TCB whose language is similar to that found in the previously discussed trade promotion agreements.

Since the PTPA entered into force at the end of October 2012, U.S. exports to Panama increased from $9.83 billion in 2012 to $10.56 billion in 2013. U.S. imports from Panama, however, decreased slightly in 2013 when compared to the year prior, though imports from Panama have still increased significantly when compared to 2011 levels: U.S. imports from Panama stood at just $389 million in 2011, spiked to $540.3 billion in 2012, and settled at $448.7 billion in 2013. While U.S. imports from Panama have fluctuated, bilateral trade between the United States and Panama has increased overall since the PTPA entered into force.

In the three fiscal years prior to 2007, the U.S. government provided some $5 million in TCB assistance to Panama, which helped to promote exports, extend trade-related business services and training, improve border security, and strengthen labor standards. This TCB program was expanded after PTPA entered into force in 2012 under the direction of the TCB committee, which itself was established as part of the PTPA. Panama's national TCB strategy focuses on sectoral adjustment strategies, since the TCB committee recognizes that certain industries are better prepared to deal with international competition while others, like agriculture, are not. The TCB committee will also pay special attention to the micro, small, and medium-sized business that make up a large portion of Panama's economy and that are likely to need the most assistance as protective trade barriers are dismantled.

Lessons Learned

Although the United States has prioritized TCB by including it in all trade agreements, outcomes can be improved significantly. In particular, policymakers must take into account who is best suited to plan, lead, and oversee TCB efforts, as well as whether TCB programs are helping all business actors, rather than just a select few.

The vast majority of TCB funding is delivered through development agencies yet these organizations are not heavily involved in the formulation of the TCB chapter in trade agreements. They are also generally unaccustomed to consulting or working directly with the private actors that trade and do business in recipient countries. U.S. TCB programs must better incorporate the operational and technical expertise of the private sector that actually moves goods in and out of developing countries and that can provide the necessary perspective and practical experience to ensure that TCB funds maximize their impact.

The development organizations also lack an account or earmark that allows for flexible, or as-needed, TCB spending to target specific countries and TCB gaps that hold back the full trade potential of developing countries, including funding reforms to adopt the WTO TFA agreement. Finally, there must be a framework that enables greater policy coordination between administrative agencies and better incorporation of private-sector and stakeholder operational expertise to set priorities, develop best practices, and design the TCB strategy. The experts on the ground, trade negotiators, and TCB implementers require an interface that allows for greater cooperation in the planning, implementation, and evaluation stages.

If trade is to lead to widespread development, it must enable entrepreneurship, rather than simply make trade easier for the well-connected elite. Building capacity for entrepreneurship is often less about improving physical infrastructure; it requires ensuring that domestic laws, regulations, and tax regimes allow a level playing field for new market entrants, and is aided by technical assistance to help businesses that have not previously traded on the international market.

4 | Conclusion and Recommendations

Trade capacity building can spur significant growth by giving developing nations a practical means to capture the benefits of increased trade and investment liberalization. Adopting comprehensive economic reforms to enhance trade performance can be difficult and costly, and targets and strategic TCB assistance can support domestic political reformers in developing countries to improve development through expanded trade. Assistance provides valuable building blocks and technical knowledge, as well as domestic political cover for potential partners. TCB cannot fundamentally alter the policy stance or condition of a government, but it can provide resources to catalyze reform to achieve deeper and more rapid change. Governments in developing countries require the resources—both financial and technical—to enact and fully implement TCB reforms, and significant U.S. support enables this process.

If a country realizes the full benefits from trade capacity reforms as reflected by expanded trade and investment opportunities for its citizens and businesses, it is more likely to pursue and support stronger trade ties in the future. A revamped and coordinate TCB strategy for the United States is necessary to capture the full range of benefits possible as negotiated in U.S. trade agreement and through U.S. trade policy. Improving trade capacity leads to increased investment, growth, and jobs and over time reduces the need for official development assistance in developing countries by supplanting aid with trade.

Improving U.S. TCB requires whole-of-government coordination, convening all the parties active in the TCB process—from goal identification to negotiation and on-the-ground implementation—including extensive consultations with the private sector and other stakeholders involved in trade in developing countries that receive TCB assistance. Improvements to TCB planning and programming would deliver significant value for the United States, as well as partner economies seeking to engage in more trade and attract additional investment. In order to improve the effectiveness and strategic value of U.S. TCB, this paper offers the following six recommendations:

1. The president should create a permanent interagency committee, which would consult with experienced private-sector advisory groups, to improve whole-of-government coordination on TCB assistance. The committee should be composed of representatives drawn from the core U.S. government agencies relevant to TCB efforts, including:

   a. U.S. Department of State

   b. U.S. Agency for International Development (USAID)

c. U.S. Trade Representative (USTR)

d. Millennium Challenge Corporation

e. U.S. Department of Commerce

f. U.S. Department of Agriculture

g. U.S. Customs and Border Protection

h. U.S. Trade and Development Agency

i. Overseas Private Investment Corporation

j. U.S. Export-Import Bank

2. The president should appoint two cochairs and one deputy to head the TCB committee. The first cochair would be the State Department's under secretary for economic growth, energy, and environment, and the second would be the deputy administrator of the U.S. Agency for International Development. The State Department is a logical choice for the cochair position, given its convening power. The State Department bridges the organizational gap between trade policy and development programming while USAID's deputy administrator would offer development and capacity-building expertise. The combination of these two cochairs would provide convening power within the U.S. government, and the ability to execute complex assistance programming, both of which are critical for a more integrated and effective U.S. approach to trade capacity building. USTR would be granted the deputy position based on its critical role in trade negotiating.

3. The interagency committee should:

    a. Agree upon a succinct and clear definition of TCB assistance.

    b. Create a set of strategic criteria and metrics used to select developing country and regional partners that would most benefit from TCB support. By establishing a selection framework, the committee provides itself a clearly bound agenda and mitigates the risk of regional priorities absorbing TCB funds without rationale, while also providing a framework for program evaluation. In addition to meeting selection criteria, countries must also demonstrate sufficient political will to effectively implement stated reforms.

4. Congress should create a line item in the Foreign Operations budget for TCB activities. This would not require new appropriations, and instead could be

achieved by coordinating and consolidating existing TCB dollars currently scattered across U.S. agency accounts. Program decisions would be made at the discretion of the interagency coordination committee, rather than independently in each implementing agency.

5. At the country level, the U.S. ambassador should be designated as the local coordinator for U.S. government-led TCB activity. He or she would work in concert with the USAID mission director, the U.S. Foreign Commercial Service, and the interagency committee to identify reform opportunities and apply TCB resources.

6. The U.S. ambassador should convene an ad hoc advisory committee, coordinated by the U.S. Commercial Service, composed primarily of private-sector representatives, both local and multinational, that are currently doing business in the country being targeted for TCB. These representatives would provide local context and expertise, and could advise on where TCB efforts and resources can be best expended.

| About the Authors

Scott Miller is a senior adviser and holds the William M. Scholl Chair in International Business at CSIS. From 1997 to 2012, Mr. Miller was director for global trade policy at Procter & Gamble, a leading consumer products company. In that position, he was responsible for the full range of international trade, investment, and business facilitation issues for the company. Mr. Miller has led many campaigns supporting U.S. free trade agreements, and as a member of numerous business associations, he has been a key contributor to international trade and investment policy. He advised the U.S. government as liaison to the U.S. Trade Representative's Advisory Committee on Trade Policy and Negotiations, as well as the State Department's Advisory Committee on International Economic Policy. Mr. Miller was the founding chairman of the Department of Commerce's Industry Trade Advisory Committee (ITAC) Investment Working Group. Earlier in his career, he was a manufacturing, marketing, and government relations executive for Procter & Gamble in the United States and Canada.

Mr. Miller was appointed to the Scholl Chair in August 2012. He holds a B.A. from Ohio Northern University and an M.A. from the University of Cincinnati College of Design, Architecture, Art, and Planning.

Daniel F. Runde is director of the Project on U.S. Leadership in Development and holds the William A. Schreyer Chair in Global Analysis at CSIS. He focuses on private enterprise development, the role of private actors in development (philanthropy, business, diasporas, and others), and the role of "emerging donors" (e.g., members of the G-20). Previously, Mr. Runde was head of the Foundations Unit for the Department of Partnerships and Advisory Service Operations at the International Finance Corporation (IFC), the private-sector arm of the World Bank Group, where he successfully positioned IFC as a partner of choice for private and corporate philanthropy. He was also responsible for leading IFC's relations with senior policymakers throughout the U.S. government. From 2005 to 2007, he was director of the Office of Global Development Alliances (GDA) at the U.S. Agency for International Development (USAID), and he led the GDA partnership initiative by providing training, networks, staff, funds, and advice to establish and strengthen alliances. His efforts leveraged $4.8 billion through 100 direct alliances and 300 others through training and technical assistance.

Earlier in his career, Mr. Runde worked for both CitiBank and BankBoston in Buenos Aires, Argentina. He started his career with Alex. Brown & Sons, Inc., in Baltimore. He was named in September 2010 as one of "40 under 40 in International Development in Washington" by the Devex Group. He is actively involved in the philanthropic sector as a member of committees for the Global Philanthropy Forum and the Committee Encouraging Corporate Philanthropy. He is a board member of the Society for International Development, the Peter C. Alderman Foundation, the Alliance for the Family, and the Advisory Boards of the UN Development Program's Growing Inclusive Markets Initiative. He has written and spoken extensively on public-private partnership issues at global conferences and symposia. Mr. Runde received an M.P.P from the Kennedy School of Government at Harvard University and a B.A., cum laude, from Dartmouth College.

C3 C3 C3 C3 C3

Charles Rice is a research assistant with the Project on Prosperity and Development, where he has worked on the roles of trade, investment, and governance in international development. Prior to joining CSIS, he worked as an English language teacher in Beijing and Yinchuan, China, for the Bainian Vocational Schools, a nonprofit vocational education program funded through the China Youth Development Foundation. Mr. Rice holds a B.S. in international political economy from the Edmund A. Walsh School of Foreign Service at Georgetown University.

Christina M. Perkins is program manager and research assistant with the Project on U.S. Leadership in Development at CSIS, where she supports research, logistics, and outreach efforts. She has contributed to a number of CSIS publications, including *Taxes and Development: The Promise of Domestic Resource Mobilization.* Prior to joining CSIS, she served as local program director with Yspaniola in the Dominican Republic, where she managed youth education and community development programs. She has also worked in communications with the Atlas Economic Research Foundation and program development with Relief International. Ms. Perkins holds a B.A. in international development studies with a minor in Spanish from the University of California at Los Angeles.